I AM A SEED OF GREATNESS

Copyright © 2018 by (Ariyan Armani Miller)

ISBN: 9781790733682

Dedication

For D'Ari

You will forever recognize your greatness.
You are a bright light of everlasting love.
I love you with all my heart.
My seed of greatness.

Mommy

I am powerful.
I am magical.
I am energetic.

I am courageous.

I am daring.

I am adventurous.

I am creative.
I am charming.
I am intelligent.

I am friendly.
I am loving.
I am sociable.

I am a winner.
I am passionate.
I am talented.

I am compassionate.

I am resplendent.

I am cheerful.

I am helpful.
I am respectful.
I am polite.

I am an entrepreneur.
I am youthful.
I am clever.

I am funny.
I am outgoing.
I am beautiful.

I am faithful.
I am thankful.
I am thoughtful.

A *message to the parents*

As parents it is our responsibility to plant seeds of greatness into our children. We must also help them understand that they themselves are seeds of greatness. I wish the best for you and your children as your journey will take you to unimaginable places.

With love and respect,

Ariyan Armani Miller

Made in the USA
Las Vegas, NV
04 September 2023